www.hmongchildrensbooks.com

Copyright © 2019 by
Kha Yang Xiong

All rights reserved. No part of this book may be reproduced or used in any manner without written permission from the copyright owner.

First printing edition
November 2019

Hardcover Book ISBN 978-1-7342450-0-4
Softcover Book ISBN 978-1-7342450-1-1

Design and Layout by Lori Sheng
Published by Hmong Children's Books

WHO ARE THE HMONG PEOPLE?

Written by Dr. Kha Yang Xiong

Dedication

This book is dedicated to all the Hmong children in the world. May you always remember your roots, culture, heritage, and language, but most of all, the warmth and kindness of the Hmong people.

Table of Contents

The History of the Hmong People 2
Where do the Hmong Live? 5
The Hmong of Laos 6
Language 8
Clothing and Jewelry 10
Hmong Clans 13
Families 14
Hmong Religions 17
Cultural Traditions 18
Food 20
Transnational Hmong 23
Glossary 24
Index 25

A Brief History of the Hmong

The origin of the Hmong people is unknown and this topic is heavily debated by **scholars**. Researchers believe that the Hmong came from the Yellow River region of China five thousand years ago. People also say that the Hmong were **oppressed** by the Han Chinese and countless lives were lost in wars and rebellions. As a result, they migrated south to parts of southern China, Laos, Vietnam, Thailand and Myanmar.

Hmong Chinese, also known as Miao, mostly live in the southern parts of China. Within this vast group, many different dialects are spoken. Some of these dialects, especially the dialects of the Hmong Chinese living closer to Laos and Vietnam, are understood by Hmong Americans.

Where do the Hmong live?

Most of the Hmong in the world live in Asia. Millions of them live in China and Vietnam. They have been farmers for thousands of years growing the food they need to survive. Their expertise is growing rice. In addition to China and Vietnam, hundreds of thousands of Hmong live in Laos, Thailand and the United States. The Hmong who live in the United States are clustered in California, Minnesota, and Wisconsin. Some Hmong live in other parts of the world, too.

COUNTRIES WHERE THE HMONG LIVE
Population Estimates

- China: 4-9 million
- Vietnam: 300K-1 million
- Laos: 200K-600K
- USA: 300K
- Thailand: 250K
- France: 15K
- Australia: 2000
- French Guiana: 1500
- Argentina: 600
- Canada: 600

The Hmong of Laos

Xob Lwm Vaj is playing a traditional instrument called a *qeej*.

An elder Hmong woman is grinding corn.

Nav Vaj (center) is wearing typical Hmong clothes from Laos.

The Hmong people living in the United States are mainly from Laos and they immigrated to the United States as a result of the Vietnam War. During the Vietnam War, the Hmong were recruited by the Central Intelligence Agency (CIA) to fight alongside the United States. Hmong soldiers helped American soldiers navigate through the thick jungles of Laos. After the United States lost the war, Americans pulled out of Laos. This left the Hmong people in danger of being killed by the communist Laotians. As a result, the United States allowed Hmong **refugees** to immigrate to America. Although, it is estimated that over 30,000 Hmong people died in the Secret War of Laos.

Language

The Hmong people have many **dialects**. The names of these dialects come from the names of the colorful clothing the Hmong women wear. The two dialects spoken by Hmong Americans are White Hmong and Green Hmong, which is also known as Mong Leng (*Moob Leeg*). They have slightly different sounds but can still be understood by both groups. In addition to sounds, Hmong dialects have tones. A tone is the change of a pitch of a sound. Say the same word with a high or low pitch and it will have two completely different meanings. For example, "pa" with a high pitch means help (*pab*) and "pa" with a low pitch means blanket (*pam*). A one-syllable word can have eight different meanings depending on the pitch that is used because there are eight tones.

TONES IN THE HMONG LANGUAGE

TONES	HMONG NAME	DESCRIPTION	VISUAL
b	Cim Siab	High	↗
m	Cim Niam	Low falling	↘
d	Cim Tod	Low rising	↪
j	Cim Ntuj	High falling	↘
v	Cim Kuv	Mid rising	↑
--	Cim Ua	Neutral	→
s	Cim Mus	Low	→
g	Cim Neeg	Breathy	✸

A VISUAL REPRESENTATION OF THE EIGHT TONES IN THE HMONG LANGUAGE

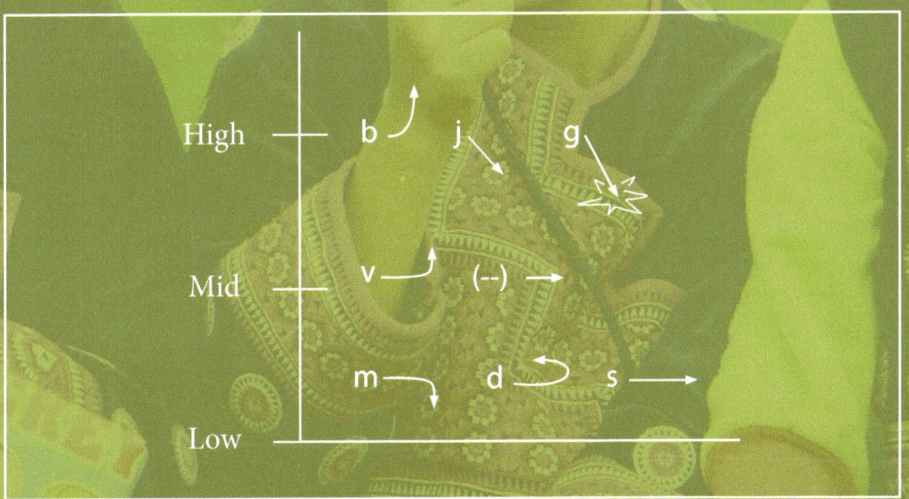

Clothing and Jewelry

Clothing is a significant aspect of the Hmong people. It is their identity. The Hmong people are most known for their needlework skills and their **textiles**. These skills have been passed down for generations and are deeply rooted in their history and culture.

Individual Hmong groups are identified by the clothing and headdress they wear. Specific needlework or textile techniques are specialized for certain groups. For example, the White Hmong are identified by their plain white skirt. The Green Hmong are most known for their colorful skirts. The Black Hmong are identified for their black jackets made from **hemp**. The Stripe Hmong have stripes on the sleeves of their jackets and the Flower Hmong have colorful jackets decorated with strings of beads.

> We are from the Black Hmong group and we use hemp to make our clothing.

Silver jewelry

In addition, the Hmong often wear silver jewelry, especially large necklaces or coins that can be rather heavy. Silver can show a person's class or wealth. The more silver an individual wears, the more wealth they own. Clothing, silver and coins are often given as a **dowry** when a young woman marries.

The Hmong in the United States do not have many opportunities to wear their traditional clothing and jewelry. They only wear them a few times a year for special occasions such as New Year's, weddings, or other events. Nowadays, Hmong clothing and jewelry in the United States are changing with imagination and creativity. The designs are expanding beyond tradition and not necessarily following typical group norms.

▼
This is a typical outfit from the Black Hmong group in Sapa, Vietnam.

Hmong Clans

Hmong people organize themselves into groups called clans. Hmong Americans are grouped into 18 clans. The **clans** are essentially their common ancestors' last names, which are shown below. Clans are like an extended family and they share a common **ancestor**. Because clans share a common ancestor, men must marry outside of their clan because the women in the clan are like their sisters. Also, when a woman gets married, she becomes part of her husband's clan. Clan members support each other in happy and difficult times. Clan leaders make important decisions and they also help families resolve problems.

Cha Tsab	**Cheng** Tsheej	**Chue** Tswb	**Fang** Faj	**Hang** Haam	**Her** Hawj
Khang Khab	**Kong** Koo	**Kue** Kwm	**Lee** Lis	**Lor** Lauj	**Moua** Muas
Pha Phab	**Thao** Thoj	**Vang** Vaj	**Vue** Vwj	**Xiong** Xyooj	**Yang** Yaj

FAMILIES

Families are very important to the Hmong people and this is reflected in their language and culture. They have rich and specific vocabulary to identify family members and these words do not exist in English. For example, a father's sister (aunt) is called a phau (*phauj*) and a mother's sister is called a niathai (*niam tais*). This is only one of many examples.

Also, Hmong people believe they are all connected in some way. When Hmong people greet each other, they will address strangers as their brothers, sisters, or aunts and uncles. Greeting a stranger as a family member brings people closer which demonstrates the warmth and community culture of the Hmong people.

Hmong boys are wearing their traditional clothing as they celebrate New Year's in Thailand.

The greater community is an extension of the family. For events such as funerals, all Hmong people attend the event even if they did not know the person who died. This is an example of how the Hmong community supports each other. Also, for other events such as weddings or the birth of a baby, all the women help cook for the celebrations. Family is an important aspect in Hmong culture and the extended family is like one's family.

Rhiav Lis, a White Hmong shaman, is performing a ceremony called *ua neeb* where she communicates with spirits in order to resolve issues. She has an assistant, Cib Yaj, who plays a drum during her voyage to the spirit world.

Paj Zeb Xyooj, a Hmong shaman is beside his altar in Laos. The altar is used for offerings, worshipping, and rituals.

Sua Lis uses chickens to help with a spirit calling ceremony, *hu plig*.

Hmong Religion

There are essentially two main religions of Hmong Americans. The first religion is **animism**. Traditional Hmong people practice animism where they believe in the spirit world and that all living things are interconnected. The Hmong believe that when a person is healthy, their spirit stays with them and when they are sick, their spirit will leave a person's side. So there are many spirit-calling ceremonies that occur in every aspect of their life from births to weddings and death. There is a healing man called a **shaman** who is able to communicate with the spiritual world and families may call him to help when sickness or other difficult issues arise. In addition, Hmong families ask for protection from their spiritual ancestors. They make offerings to their ancestors to keep them safe and healthy.

The other religion is Christianity. Christian Hmong believe in God. They attend church to listen to the word of God preached by a **pastor**. Christian Hmong want to share the **gospel** with others and they participate in church activities and events in their community.

Cultural Traditions

In Laos, the Hmong were mainly farmers. After the harvesting season, when food is abundant and there is time to rest before the next planting cycle, the Hmong celebrate the coming new year. New Year's is an important event and women and girls spend an entire year making their beautiful embroidery (*paj ntaub*) outfits to wear during the New Year celebration. During this event, young adults dress up and play a game where they toss a cloth ball to each other. This game also includes singing traditional songs call *kwv txhiaj*. New Year games and activities encourage interaction, so the celebrations have become a typical courting time for young adults to find a marriage partner. Although, Hmong Americans mostly live in cities, they still celebrate the new year celebrations.

▶ Hmong youth are participating in a traditional ball tossing activity during a New Year's celebration in Laos.

Also during the new year celebrations and other times of the year, Hmong people perform a traditional custom called spirit-calling or *hu plig*. As mentioned earlier, they believe that sometimes the soul may leave the body and cause people to be sick. Spirit-calling ensures that the souls have safely returned to their homes and their bodies which promotes good health. During these spirit-calling ceremonies, chickens are used to help find the spirits and lead them back to their homes and families. Families typically perform spirit-calling ceremonies at the end of the year to ensure that the new year will be healthy and lucky. After the ceremonies, Hmong families enjoy a hearty meal with family and friends.

FOOD

Traditionally, Hmong people in **agricultural** societies ate whatever they grew on their farms and from the animals they raised, trapped, or hunted. Their simple meals included rice, corn, squash, cucumber and a variety of other vegetables, mainly leafy greens and fresh herbs. On special occasions, they would have some meat with their meals, mainly pork and chicken and sometimes beef and fish. They also drink a clear soup or tea made from squash or pumpkin called *zaub tsuag* during their meals. The Hmong also have a pickled dish made from mustard

greens called *zaub pos* or *zaub qaub*. As the Hmong migrated to other countries, they were influenced by other cultures. For example, the Hmong in America have been influenced by the food from Southeast Asia. They use many fresh herbs and spices to season their food, some of which include ginger, green onions, cilantro, chilies, garlic and mint. These spices help make Hmong food very flavorful. This is why spicy chilies are served at the table with main dishes of rice, vegetables and meat. Some favorite dishes include fresh free-range chicken, spicy papaya salad, delicious egg rolls, larb, curry noodle soup, pho soup, barbecued pork and Hmong sausage.

Two Hmong American girls are graduating from the University of Colorado Denver.

Transnational Hmong

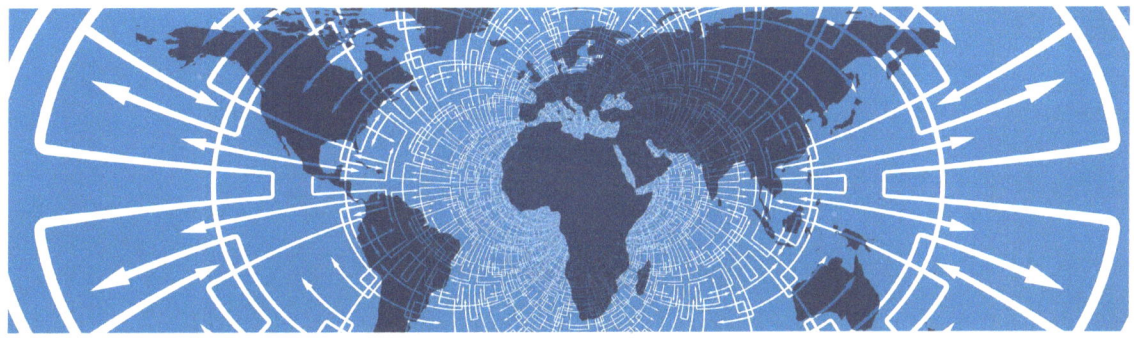

Hmong people around the world are able to connect and communicate through different forms of media. With the advancement of technology and the Internet, Hmong people from all over the world are learning about each other. For example, Hmong Americans research their roots and their distant relatives in China and other parts of the world. Many discoveries are being made, including historical aspects. Also, when the Hmong first arrived to the United States from a mostly agricultural society, they did not have much experience in **academic** settings. Now, Hmong individuals are earning advanced college degrees and have many professional careers. More people are beginning to know about the Hmong and their impactful contributions to their communities and societies.

Glossary

Academics-having to do with school

Agricultural-farming

Ancestor-relatives that have passed away such as grandparents

Animism-belief that living things have spirits

Clan-a group of families or people of similar interest

Dialect-a form of language specific to a region

Dowry-property or money brought by a bride to her husband on their marriage.

Gospel-the teaching of Christ

Hemp-the fiber from a cannabis plant used for making fabric, rope or paper

Oppressed-to treat unfairly or with cruelty

Pastor-a teacher of the Bible

Refugee-a person forced to leave their country due to war or disaster

Scholar- a person who has a lot of knowledge about a particular topic

Shaman-a spiritual healer

Textile-a type of cloth or fabric

Transnational-involving more than one nation or country

INDEX

America, 7

Ancestor, 13, 17

Animism, 17

China, 2, 3, 5, 23

Christian, 17

Clans, 13

Clothing, 7, 10, 11, 12, 15, 18

Dialects, 3, 8

Dowry, 11

Family, 13, 14, 15, 17, 19

Food, 19, 20, 21

Gospel, 17

Hmong language, 3, 8, 9, 14

Hmong Chinese, 3

Laos, 2, 3, 5, 7, 16, 18, 19

New Year, 11, 15, 18, 19

Refugee, 17

Religion, 16, 17

Shaman, 11

Secret War, 7

Spirit Calling, 16, 17

Tones, 8, 9

United States, 5, 7, 11, 23

Acknowledgements

A special thank you to teachers and friends who took the time to preview the book and offer meaningful suggestions and insights. Also, thank you to Victoria Vorreiter at www.tribalmusicasia.com for her donation of photos from Laos and Thailand. Finally, a heart-warm thank you to Lori Sheng for supporting this book with a generous donation of her graphic designing skills and expertise.

Photo Credits

The publisher is grateful to the following for permission to reproduce material:
Cover@ChatraweeWiratgasem/Shutterstock, Table of contents@Pixabay, p.3@plus99/Bigstock, 2390890985MSH/Pixabay, p.4@ledo/Shutterstock
p.6&7@ VictoriaVorreiter, p.10@VictoriaVorreiter, p.11@kyxiong, RoseHanse,
p.9 Amornpant Kookaki / Shutterstock,
p.12@Pixabay, p.14@Digitalpress/Bigstock, p.15@themorningglory/Bigstock,
p.16@VictoriaVorreiter, p.18@ATstudio/Bigstock, p.19@Pixabay, p.20@SubinPumson/Bigstock, Engdao/Bigstock, p.21@Engdao/Bigstock,
p.22@kyxiong, p.23@geralt/Pixabay, Back Cover@R.M.Nunes/Bigstock

About the Author

Dr. Kha Yang Xiong was born in a Hmong village in the hills of Laos. At the end of the Vietnam War, her family fled to escape persecution and settled in the refugee camps of Thailand. When she was seven years old, her family immigrated to the United States. Currently, Kha is a teacher helping children learn English. She recently received her doctorate degree from the University of Colorado Denver with a focus on equity in education. She is passionate about helping children learn about their roots, culture, heritage, and language. Kha is on a journey to make books to teach about the Hmong people.

www.ingramcontent.com/pod-product-compliance
Lightning Source LLC
LaVergne TN
LVHW071029070426
835507LV00002B/90